D1241272

Alan, Enjoy reading about
your second love.
Always,
Emma

THE PLEASURES OF WINES AND SPIRITS

ABERCROMBIE & FITCH

LIBRARY

BOOKSELLERS
EST. 1892

Introduction

"Let us have wine and women, mirth and laughter, sermons and soda water the day after."

Don Juan, First Canto, Lord Byron

If you bought this book, you cannot be a teetotaller, therefore the pleasures will be obvious, and need no real introduction. The noble grape and the grain have been praised and applauded by diverse writers, some experts, some merely afficionados, for centuries. Dipping into countless volumes choosing "bon mots" on the subject is rather like a wine-tasting, just sampling a little of those special indulgences. Whether a romantic rendezvous with someone special or in more raucous company, any occasion can be an excuse to imbibe.

Studies into the history of production and social uses of wines and spirits have nowadays almost become an art form. But the social habits and daily timetables are perhaps the major change – apart from technology – over the last few hundred years. On this romp through literature, it seems that in the eighteenth and nineteenth centuries, it was popular to drink punch, concocted from lethal mixtures of strong spirits, whereas in the twentieth century, these are more usually replaced by cocktails or aperitifs. Put simply, our forebears drank *far* more! Indeed, with the recent obsessions with health and diet, an excess of spirits is considered bad for you, although whisky is said to be beneficial for arthritis, and red wine for the heart – *in moderation* of course. Even medical statistics indicate this can be so.

This selection takes us through a drinking day: first, an aperitif before lunch or dinner, perhaps a "pastis" or martini at your favourite cafe when visiting Paris or Rome? Tastes bring back locations and memories, but foreign drinks are often never quite the same back home. Sherry, although an aperitif in its own right, and delicious when drunk iced in southern Spain, used to be more popular than today, and was often drunk with the first course at formal dinners. Indeed, at such a table, counting the glasses accompanying each course can be most impressive, ranging from sherries, to white wine, red wine, dessert wine, brandy, liqueurs, or port. Auberon Waugh wrote that "women still regard port as their natural enemy" and never, even in our more emancipated days, was a truer word spoken. For after dinner, in Victorian and Edwardian days, the women were banished to more genteel conservation, while the gentlemen remained at table, passing the port and discussing politics or sport, passing the port and putting the world to rights, passing the port, gossiping and telling jokes, and passing the port . . .

Champagne of course is in a class of its own, and the legend that the discovery of the secret of its manufacture prompted Dom Perignon to cry out that he was "drinking the stars" is no less believable today.

It is said that "a meal without wine is like a day without sunshine." Here, more than anywhere in the literature of drink, adjectives such as "velvet" or "fruity" abound, amidst claims of the *great year*, the *first-class* vintage. It all depends if you just wish to enjoy, or collect and lay down wine for the future, as investment. George Saintsbury wrote that "If Claret is the Queen of natural wines, Burgundy is the King" and despite rival claims, this remains so. But each to his own palate: at a recent wine-tasting an enthusiast was heard to rhapsodize about the "bouquet of cats and gooseberry bushes" which, as it turned out, was a compliment!

After dinner, the formal toast before the speeches was, and still is, a ritual to be observed. Here beginneth the legless stage perhaps . . . Thereafter, more liqueurs, or brandy, with or without soda, before a final nightcap – another glass of that delicious ten-year old Malt before turning in?

Jenny de Gex, 1991

APÉRITIFS

Soda-water should never be mixed with the most popular and violent apéritifs, which are generically called 'pastis' or 'anis.' They are made by secret processes and are generally green (but the Greek equivalent, ouzo, is white and some Provençal home-made pastis is orange). When in bottle they are clear, but as soon as water is put with them they become cloudy. They taste of aniseed, and until you are used to them they have a violently stimulating effect. They are among the most questionable and habit-forming drinks known to man, and in their strongest forms are forbidden even in France. In their original strengths they were called absinthes, and contained wormwood, which is proveably a deleterious substance.

The Plain Man's Guide to Wine, Raymond Postgate, 1951

Sherry: A Self-Willed Wine

Sherry is a self-willed wine which gives a good deal of trouble to its guardians during its early years: it must have its own way, but, like many a difficult child, when Sherry reaches the age of sweet reasonableness, it is the most amenable of all wines, the only one that will not let its nose be put out by being left overnight and even for some days in a decanter; the only one to put up cheerfully with cigarette smoke and over-scented women.

A Wine Primer, André Simon, 1946

Paul-Chabas

Punch Drunk

'The Doctor stood over his victims, victorious. He had taken, singly more punch than any three of them together; yet there they all lay helpless, while he was steady of hand and speech.

"Gentlemen, I perceive that I have been for some time talking to a sleeping audience. Swine of Circe, I drink to your headaches in the morning."'

Sir W. Besant

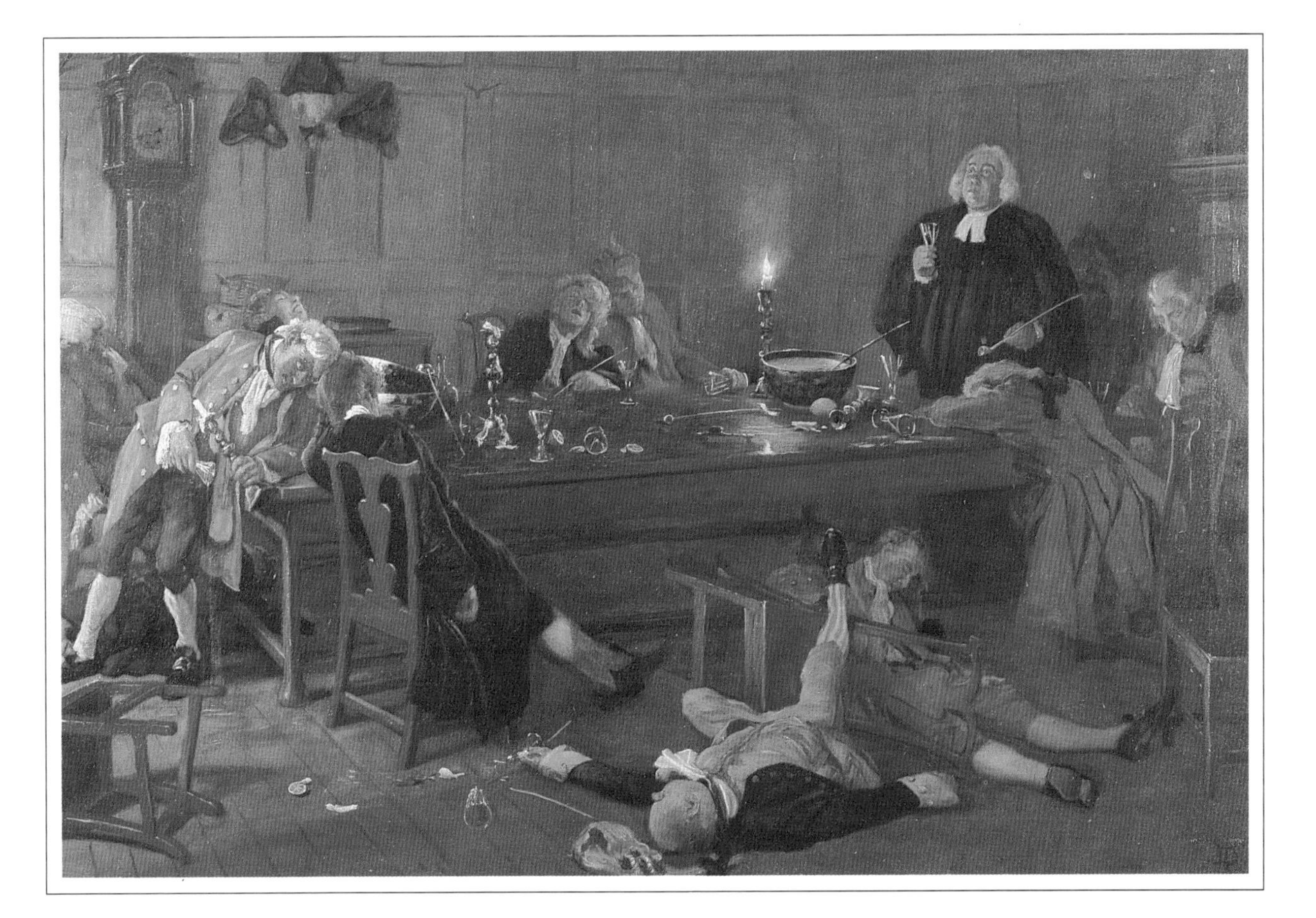

Ingredients For Punch

Buck paid me his Tithe but did not dine with us. Mr. Heming came in the Afternoon and spent the Afternoon and Evening with us. Nancy dined in the Study to day by herself. We had for Dinner, Salt Fish, a Leg of Mutton boiled and Capers, boiled and rost Beef and plenty of plumb and plain Puddings – Punch, Wine and Strong Beer after Dinner. There was six Bottles of Rum made into Punch, 3 Bowls, 2 Bottles of Rum in each. There was seven Bottles of Wine – great Quantities of strong Beer – 9 Lemons – 1 P^{d} and ½ of Sugar and half a Pound of Tobacco made use of.

The Diary of a Country Parson 1758-1802, James Woodforde,
(selected and edited by John Beresford, 1935)

A Drink with Something in It

There is something about a Martini,
A tingle remarkably pleasant;
A yellow, a mellow Martini;
I wish that I had one at present.
There is something about a Martini,
Ere the dining and dancing begin,
And to tell you the truth,
It is not the vermouth –
I think that perhaps it's the gin.

Collected Verse From 1929 On, Ogden Nash

CAFE
RESTAURANT
Jean Béraud.

CHAMPAGNE

Champagne is for cheer, for formality. Champagne, and only champagne, is an adequate potable for the Special Occasion when an engagement is announced, or a marriage culminated – when you have sold your first book, been made a partner in the firm, or written a successful play, broken par, or own a Derby winner – or been granted a divorce, or become a father. It is drunk because you desire to usher in the New Year properly, or when you drink a toast to the sainted Robert Burns or Guy Fawkes. An ingenious citizen can manufacture a reason for tippling champagne at the drop of a magnum, but the drinking thereof should be delightfully formal, spiced with a little spurious dignity, predicated on traditional formulae.

Esquire Drink Book, edited by F. A. Birmingham, 1957

The Sparkling Touch

'You know my way with the women; champagne's the thing; make 'em drink, make 'em talk; – make 'em talk, make 'em do anything.'

The Paris Sketch Book, William Makepeace Thackeray, 1840

In The Name of Bacchus

A man who sets you down to a driblet of champagne – who gives you a couple of beggarly glasses between the courses, and winks to John who froths up the liquor in your glass, and screws up the remainder of the bottle for his master's next day's drinking – such a man is an impostor and despicable snob . . . If money is an object to you, drink water . . . but if there is to be champagne, have no stint of it, in the name of Bacchus . . . When people have had plenty of champagne, they fancy they have been treated liberally. If you wish to save, save upon your hocks, sauternes, and moselles, which count for nothing, but disappear down careless throats like so much toast and water . . .

Incomparably the best champagne I know is to be found in England. It is the most doctored, the most brandied, the most barley-sugared, the most *winy* wine in the world.

Miscellaneous Papers, William Makepeace Thackeray, 1885

Champers à Deux

For two intimates, lovers or comrades, to spend a quiet evening with a magnum, drinking no apéritif before, nothing but a glass of cognac after – that is the ideal . . . The worst time is that dictated by convention, in a crowd, in the early afternoon, at a wedding reception.

New York *Vogue*, Evelyn Waugh, 1937

Thy Explosive Cork

The sound of thy explosive cork, Champagne, has, by some strange witchery, of a sudden taught men the sweet music of speech. A murmur as of a rising storm runs round the table: badinage commences, flirtations flourish . . . We might tell of breakfasts, and of suppers, suddenly converted from Saharas of intolerable dullness into oases of smiles and laughter by the appearance of Champagne.

Wit, Wisdom and Morals, Distilled from Bacchus, Charles Tovey

WINES

Wine is one of the most civilized things in the world and one of the natural things of the world that has been brought to the greatest perfection, and it offers a greater range for enjoyment and appreciation than, possibly, any other purely sensory thing.

Death in the Afternoon, Ernest Hemingway, 1932

A. MAREILHAC & Cie
BORDEAUX

A Serious Acquaintance With Wine

We would sit, he and I, in the Painted Parlour with three bottles open on the table and three glasses before each of us; Sebastian had found a book on wine-tasting, and we followed its instructions in detail. We warmed the glass slightly at a candle, filled a third of it, swirled the wine round, nursed it in our hands, held it to the light, breathed it, sipped it, filled our mouths with it and rolled it over the tongue, ringing it on the palate like a coin on a counter, tilted our heads back and let it trickle down the throat. Then we talked of it and nibbled Bath Oliver biscuits, and passed on to another wine; then back to the first, then on to another, until all three were in circulation and the order of glasses got confused, and we fell out over which was which, and we passed the glasses to and fro between us until there were six glasses, some of them with mixed wines in them which we had filled from the wrong bottle, till we were obliged to start again with three clean glasses each, and the bottles were empty and our praise of them wilder and more exotic.

". . . It is a little, shy wine like a gazelle."

"Like a leprechaun."

"Dappled, in a tapestry meadow."

"Like a flute by still water."

". . . And this is a wise old wine."

"A prophet in a cave."

". . . And this is a necklace of pearls on a white neck."

"Like a swan."

"Like the last unicorn."

And we would leave the golden candle-light of the dining-room for the star-light outside and sit on the edge of the fountain, cooling our hands in the water and listening drunkenly to its splash and gurgle over the rocks.

"Ought we to be drunk *every* night?" Sebastian asked one morning.

"Yes, I think so."

"I think so too."

Brideshead Revisited, Evelyn Waugh, 1945

A Draught of Sunshine

Hence Burgundy, Claret, and Port,
Away with old Hock and Madeira,
Too earthly ye are for my sport;
There's a beverage brighter and clearer.
Instead of a pitiful rummer,
My wine overbrims a whole summer;
My bowl is the sky,
And I drink at my eye,
Till I feel in the brain
A Delphian pain –
Then follow, my Caius! then follow:
On the green of the hill
We will drink our fill
Of golden sunshine,
Till our brains intertwine
With the glory and grace of Apollo!
God of the Meridian,
And of the East and West,
To thee my soul is flown,
And my body is earthward press'd.

John Keats, 1795-1821

Women, Love, and Wine!

The murm'ring brook, the fanning breeze,
Gay myrtles, flow'ry banks, and trees,
To doat on some incline;
But nobler blessings I advise,
The greatest joys below the skies
Are women, love, and wine!

From scene to scene, while thousands rove,
Unless by women, wine, and love,
In secret let them pine;
When I the world with pleasure tell,
We may all ev'ry care dispel
With women, love, and wine!

The restless wretch, who doats on gold,
And would in flames the world behold,
To see his treasure shine,
Shall gen'rous grow, his self despise,
Be happy, joyous, honest, wise,
With women, love, and wine!

May youth and age, of all degrees,
On such inspiring comfort seize,
'Twill every sense refine;
To see mankind so nobly blest,
Superior pow'rs shall wish to taste
Of women, love, and wine!

Anon.

True Connoisseurs

As long as the wine is in the mouth, one receives a pleasant but indistinct impression; it is only when one has finished swallowing it that one can really taste, appreciate and identify its particular bouquet; and a short while must elapse before the gourmand can say: 'It's good, or passable, or bad. Bless my soul! It's Chambertin! Good grief! It's Suresnes!' . . .

True connoisseurs *sip* their wine; for as they pause after each mouthful, they obtain the sum total of pleasure they would have experienced had they emptied the glass at a single draught.

La Physiologie du goût, Brillat-Savarin, 1828

Choosing the Wine

Red bordeaux is like the lawful wife: an excellent beverage that goes with every dish and enables one to enjoy one's food. But now and then a man wants a change . . .

My Life and Loves, Frank Harris, 1922–27

WINE SNOB

The alcohol in wine is as the canvas upon which an artist paints a picture. . . . It is not the small percentage of alcohol that appeals to you, but the brilliant ruby of the wine's colour, the attractive perfume of its bouquet and the delicious savour of its farewell, the lingering taste which it leaves behind as it descends smoothly down your grateful throat.

A Wine Primer, André Simon, 1946

Reasons to be Cheerful

At the first cup man drinks wine, at the second wine drinks wine, at the third wine drinks man.

Japanese Proverb

Let us drink to have wit, not to destroy it.

Panard, 18th-century French poet

Wine hath drowned more men than the sea.

Thomas Fuller, 17th century

Drink and Drive Care Away

Wine is the liquor of life,
The heart is consumed by care,
Good fellows, then, end the strife
'Twixt the bottle and despair.
Derry, down, derry,
Hey down, derry.

Drinking Song, G. Colman, Senior

Club Drinking

Bacchus is the divinity to whom Waggle devotes his especial worship. "Give me wine, my boy," says he to his friend Wiggle, who is prating about lovely woman; and holds up his glass full of the rosy fluid, and winks at it portentously, and sips it, and smacks his lips after it, and meditates on it, as if he were the greatest of connoisseurs.

I have remarked this excessive wine-amateurship especially in youth. Snoblings from college, Fledglings from the army, Goslings from the public schools, who ornament our Clubs, are frequently to be heard in great force upon wine questions. "This bottle's corked," says Snobling; and Mr. Sly, the butler, taking it away, returns presently with the same wine in another jug, which the young amateur pronounces excellent. "Hang champagne!" says Fledgling; "it's only fit for gals and children. Give me pale sherry at dinner, and my twenty-three claret afterwards." "What's port now?" says Gosling; "disgusting thick sweet stuff – where's the old dry wine one *used* to get?" Until the last twelvemonth, Fledgling drank small-beer at Doctor Swishtail's; and Gosling used to get his dry old port at a gin-shop in Westminster – till he quitted that seminary, in 1844.

The Book of Snobs, William Makepeace Thackeray, 1869

Gerard Portielje

AFTER DINNER

'Gentlemen, – in rising – propose toast about to give – feel werry – feel werry (Yorkshireman, "werry muzzy?") J. – feel werry – (Mr. Spiers "werry sick?") J. – werry – (Crane, "werry thirsty?") J. – feel werry – (Nimrod, "werry wise?") J. – no; but werry *sensible* – great compliment – eyes of England upon us – give you the health – Mr. H'Apperley Nimrod – three times three!'

He then attempted to rise for the purpose of marking the time, but his legs deserted his body, and, after two or three lurches, down he went with a tremendous thump under the table. He called first for 'Batsay,' then for 'Binjimin,' and, game to the last, blurted out, 'Lift me up! – tie me in my chair! – fill my glass!'

Jorrocks Jaunts and Jollities, R. S. Surtees, 1874

PASSING THE PORT

'Do you drink port or claret, Mr Sponge?' asked Jawleyford, preparing to push whichever he preferred over to him.

'I'll take a little port, *first*, if you please,' replied our friend – as much as to say, 'I'll finish off with claret.'

'You'll find that very good, I expect,' said Mr Jawleyford, passing the bottle to him; 'it's '20 wine – very rare wine to get now – was a very rich fruity wine, and was a long time before it came into drinking. Connoisseurs would give any money for it.'

'It has still a good deal of body,' observed Sponge, turning off a glass and smacking his lips, at the same time holding the glass up to the candle to see the oily mark it made on the side.

'Good sound wine – good sound wine,' said Mr Jawleyford, 'Have plenty lighter, if you like.' The light wine was made by watering the strong.

'Oh, no, thank you,' replied Mr Sponge, 'Oh, no, thank you. I like good strong military port.'

'So do I,' said Mr Jawleyford, 'so do I; only unfortunately it doesn't like me – am obliged to drink claret. When I was in the Bumperkin yeomanry we drank nothing but port.'

Mr Sponge's Sporting Tour, R. S. Surtees, 1853

A Fine Vintage

By the time the ladies took their departure, Mr. Jawleyford had somewhat recovered from the annoyance of his disappointment; and as they retired he rang the bell, and desired Spigot to set in the horse-shoe table, and bring a bottle of the 'green seal,' being the colour affixed on the bottles of a four-dozen hamper of port ('curious old port at 48s.') that had arrived from 'Wintle & Co.' by rail (goods train of course) that morning.

'There!' exclaimed Jawleyford, as Spigot placed the richly cut decanter on the horse-shoe table. 'There!' repeated he, drawing the green curtain as if to shade it from the fire but in reality to hide the dulness the recent shaking had given it; 'that wine,' said he, 'is a quarter of a century in bottle, at the very least.'

'Indeed,' observed Sponge: 'time it was drunk.'

'A quarter of a century?' gaped Robert Foozle.

'Quarter of a century if it's a day,' replied Jawleyford, smacking his lips as he set down his glass after imbibing the precious beverage.

'Very fine,' observed Sponge; adding, as he sipped off his glass, 'it's odd to find such old wine so full-bodied.'

Mr Sponge's Sporting Tour, R. S. Surtees, 1853

G-G-GREEN CHARTREUSE

Anthony had lost his stammer in the deep waters of his old romance. It came floating back to him, momentarily, with the coffee and liqueurs. “Real G-g-green Chartreuse, made before the expulsion of the monks. There are five distinct tastes as it trickles over the tongue. It is like swallowing a sp-spectrum.

Brideshead Revisited, Evelyn Waugh, 1945

The Liqueur

They are also, being as a rule both too strong and too sweet, the most questionably wholesome; and excess in them results in sufferings the most unpleasant of all such sufferings. Nor do they possess the natural grace and charm – the almost intellectual as well as sensual interest – of the best wine. On the other hand, they are for the most part very pleasant to the taste; they are frequently very pretty to look at; and if there be any truth in the old and perhaps somewhat rash statement as to the connection between the wills or wishes of womankind and of the Divinity, they cannot be hateful to God. For nearly all ladies, and especially all young ladies, like them very much indeed.

Notes on a Cellar-Book, George Saintsbury, 1920

Jean Béraud

The Scotch Tradition

On special occasions, too, like lamb sales or Cattle Show Day, almost the whole community used to go what was known locally as 'on the batter'. Then nearly everyone from the doctors, the staid elders of the Kirk, and sometimes a minister, to the humblest farm hand or tinker imbibed freely. Tongues were loosed and stories swapped, and kinsman gave kinsman the news of a whole year with the detailed exactitude of men who, in those days of slow transport, lived far apart and saw one another rarely. Admittedly at the end of the day the trail home was often wobbly, but I do not think that much harm came from these meetings. They brought a scattered community together, gave it consciousness of its cohesion, and fostered good fellowship. They were, too, a reaction against puritanism and the drabness of daily life. I remember a Highland saying of those days: 'One whisky is all right, two is too much, and three is too few.' Two makes you want another and after three you can't stop.

Scotch, Sir Robert Bruce Lockhart, 1951

ACKNOWLEDGEMENTS

PICTURE CREDITS

Front cover: *Mr Pickwick Addressing His Friends*, Charles Green (Bridgeman Art Library/Dickens House Museum, London)
Title page: *The Bar at the Folies Bergeres*, Edouard Manet (Courtauld Institute Galleries, London)

4 (Mary Evans Picture Library)
5 *M. Boileau in a Cafe, 1893*, Henri de Toulouse-Lautrec (Bridgeman/Cleveland Museum of Art, Ohio)
6 (Mary Evans Picture Library)
7 *The Corner of the Table*, Paul Chabas (Giraudon/Musée des Beaux-Arts, Tourcoing)
9 *The Reverend G. Shovel*, Thomas Davidson (Christopher Wood Gallery)
11 *Mr Oldham and Guests*, Joseph Highmore (Tate Gallery, London)
12 *Au Café*, Oscar Wilson (Fine Art Photographs)
13 *Paris, Le Café de la Paix*, Jean Beraud (Fine Art Photographs)
15 *Hip Hip Hurrah! Artists' Party, Skagen*, Peter Severin Kroyer (Bridgeman/Goteborgs Konstmuseum, Sweden)
16 (Mary Evans Picture Library)
17 *The Champagne Bar*, Alfred Bastien (Bridgeman/Whitford & Hughes, London)
19 *Tagg's Island*, Sir Alfred Munnings (Sir Alfred Munnings Art Museum, Dedham)
21 *Chez Père Lathuille*, Edouard Manet (Scala/Musée des Beaux-Arts, Tournai)
22 (Mary Evans Picture Library)
23 *Dinner with Friends*, Josef Engelhard (Bridgeman/Historisches Museum der Stadt, Vienna)
24 *A Basket of Grapes*, Thomas Keyse (Bridgeman/Private Collection)
25 *A Promising Vintage*, Jan Moerman (Fine Art Photographs/Gavin Graham Gallery)
27 *Still Life of Fruit and Glass*, Edward Ladell (Fine Art Photographs)
29 *Afternoon in Fiesole*, Marie Baccio Bacci (Scala/Uffizi Gallery, Florence)
31 *Au Cafe*, Fernand Toussaint (Bridgeman/Whitford & Hughes)
33 *The Artists' Breakfast*, Peter Severin Kroyer (Bridgeman/Skagens Museum, Denmark)
34 (Mary Evans Picture Library)
35 *Bank Holiday*, William Strang (Tate Gallery, London)
36 *A Still Life of a Wine Glass, Jugs, Grapes & Flowers*, Magnus Peterson (Fine Art Photographs)
37 *Mr Woodbridge and Captain Holland*, William Hogarth (Bridgeman/Agnew & Sons, London)
39 *One For the Road*, Henry Gillard Glindoni (Bridgeman/J. Collins & Son Fine Paintings, Devon)
40 (Mary Evans Picture Library)
41 *Lefranc, Marchand de Vin, Boulevard de Clichy, Paris*, Eero Jarnefelt (Bridgeman/Athenaeum Museum, Helsinki)
43 *A Fine Vintage*, Gerard Portielje (Bridgeman/Christie's, London)
45 *Mr Pickwick Addressing His Friends*, Charles Green (Bridgeman/Dickens House Museum, London)
47 *A Corner of the Table, Paris, 1872*, Henri Fantin Latour (Bridgeman/Musée d'Orsay, Paris)
48 *The Butler's Glass*, Walter Dendy Sadler (Fine Art Photographs)
49 *A Good Vintage*, Gerard Portielje (Bridgeman/Private Collection)
50 (Mary Evans Picture Library)
51 *The Cafe Royal, London 1912*, Sir William Orpen (Bridgeman/Giraudon/Musée d'Orsay, Paris)
52 (Punch)
53 *Dinner at the Ambassadeurs*, Jean Beraud (Bridgeman/Giraudon/Musée Carnavalet, Paris)
54 (Mary Evans Picture Library)
55 *His Favourite Table*, George Broughton (Bridgeman/King Street Galleries, London)

TEXT CREDITS

Text extracts from the following sources are reprinted with the kind permission of the publishers and copyright holders stated. Should any copyright holder have been inadvertently omitted they should apply to the publishers who will be pleased to credit them in any subsequent editions.

4 Raymond Postgate, *The Plain Man's Guide to Wine* (Michael Joseph, 1951 © Professor Raymond Postgate)
6, 36: Andrew Simon, *A Wine Primer* (Michael Joseph, 1946)
12 Ogden Nash, *I Wouldn't Have Missed It* (Andre Deutsch; Curtis Brown Inc, USA)
14 *The Esquire Drink Book* (edited by Frederic A. Birmingham, Esquire magazine, 1957, Frederick Muller Ltd)
20 Evelyn Waugh, *New York Vogue 1937*
26, 50: Evelyn Waugh, *Brideshead Revisited 1945* (reprinted by permission of the Peters Fraser & Dunlop Group Ltd.)
24 Ernest Hemingway, *Death In the Afternoon* (Jonathan Cape, The Estate of Ernest Hemingway, copyright 1932 Charles Scribner's Sons; renewed © 1960 by Ernest Hemingway)
38 Robin Don, *The Compleat Imbiber* (Gilbey Vintners, 1971)
54 Sir Robert Bruce Lockhart, *Scotch* (Bodley Head, 1951)

First published in Great Britain 1991 for
ABERCROMBIE & FITCH, INC.
by Pavilion Books Limited
196 Shaftesbury Avenue, London WC2H 8JL

Designed by Andrew Barron & Collis Clements Associates

A CIP catalogue record for this book is available from the British Library

ISBN 1-85145-810-7

Printed and bound in Scotland by Eagle Colour Books